MEMOIRS OF A FORGETFUL MIND

MEMOIRS OF A FORGETFUL MIND

Donna Dedier James

True to life comedic dramas and forgetful stories, providing a glimpse inside the workings of the brain of one unassuming individual, giving you the opportunity for a hearty dose of what has been described as '...the best medicine.'

LINC Publishing House 2014
South Ozone Park, NY USA

All rights reserved
Copyright © 2014 Donna C Dedier James
Cover Design & Photos: Donna Dedier James
Interior Design & Illustrations: Donna Dedier James

ISBN: 069223571X
ISBN-13: 978-0692235713

No part of this publication may be reproduced or transmitted in any form or by any means, electronic or mechanical, including photocopying, recording or any information storage and retrieval system now known or to be invented, without the prior written permission of the copyright owner and the publisher.

For further ordering information please visit us online at
www.wilaf.com

Printed in the U.S.A.

This book is dedicated to you:

My husband Neil - you stuck it out all these years, in spite of my craziness. Your great cooking and support went a long way to making this possible.
My precious Akeyla (wise one) - we have been blessed to have you. What a tremendous support you proved to be to our family, as a sister twice over, and a daughter, in ways too numerous to mention.
My son, Yohance Ayodele (joy enters the house), our first gift from God, and true to the meaning of your name, you keep us laughing.
My grown, baby sister, Arlene - you kept pushing me.
Thanks Antoni - you got me going.

CONTENTS

Chapter 1............Drug Pusher

Chapter 2............Get It Off me

Chapter 3............Was Not Lost But Was Found

Chapter 4............Bag Of Books

Chapter 5............Three Strips

Chapter 6............No Friends

Chapter 7............Belching Smoke

Chapter 8............Chinese

Chapter 9............Keys

Chapter 10..........Casing

Chapter 11..........Hold On

Chapter 12..........Delivery

Chapter 13..........Stand Clear of The Closing Doors

Chapter 14..........Tickets

Chapter 15..........Bridge Over Very Cold Waters

Chapter 16..........Break In

Chapter 17..........Come Out With Your Hands Up

All my life I have forgotten things; yes, including my children. So when my son in law, Antoni, said to me: "Ma you should write a book and call it 'Memoirs of a Forgetful Mind," I took his advice.

I put my other book on hold, and put some of my stories together.

It seems my existence is comical, so hey, I am happy if my `sanity' contributes to others' joy. Since they seem to be constantly entertained by my actions, though hardly ever intentional on my part, why not you?

Some are funny, some are downright crazy but aren't we all kind of crazy in some kind of way? It's that craziness that makes each one of us unique. Go ahead and laugh, because in some small way, one of these might just relate to your life too.

June 16, 2014

MEMOIRS OF A
FORGETFUL MIND

Chapter One

The graceful arrival of summer was invigorating. With dark, shiny, sun-baked face devoid of emotions, Justin walked into the yard and headed towards their apartment door.

He was staying with his grandmother and grandfather, the owners of the property, our landlord and landlady. They occupied the ground floor, another family the first floor, and we the second.

Teenage years were proving to be a real challenge for Justin. His grandmother was doing the best she could to help him get his act together. He seemed to have some issues but no one knew for sure whether it was associated with the drugs with which he was dabbling, or if it was indeed a mental health problem.

His grandmother was a buoyant, kind hearted individual, always looking for ways to help. She always greeted you with a big smile and a big hug. More important to her reputation was her genuine love and devotion to her God. Unmistakable, was the fervor with which she attempted to carry out her responsibility as a true follower of the Christ and a loyal servant of his heavenly father.

It was her love of God that spilled over onto love of neighbor; evidently, it also impacted her undeniable love for her husband. Gentle and mild were perfect descriptions for her tone of voice, and one could not help but notice the endearing terms she always used when speaking to him, and about him.

Don't be fooled by this. She was as firm as could be when needed; for this reason you could depend on her to give you her unbiased view of any situation under discussion. She was always 'straight up.'

His grandfather was very jovial, and always ready to lend a helping hand to one and all. Entrepreneurship coursed through his veins. Real estate for him was second nature.

His wife's ability was also nothing short of amazing having been involved in almost every occupation and business under the sun.

She was in the army national guard reserve, worked as a security guard, a postal worker, city bus driver, almost became a nurse, had a cleaning business, been a butcher, real estate broker, elder care aide, day-care owner, owned and operated a group home. In a nut shell it can be said she was: "a butcher, perhaps even a baker, not sure if she got to the point of being a candle stick maker"... got the picture?

Food in that household was a plenty, and family dining out was a monthly occasion. Justin had nothing short of a good life. The annual vacation was another one of their family's indulgences supported by his mother's hearty income. Lend me his life for a couple of years, pleeeaassse.

And so it was that day, upon opening the front door and heading downstairs into what should have been a beautiful day, when I caught sight of Justin.

As my right shoe landed on the second stair my glance

Drug Pusher

past him brought into vision the disturbing sight of a stranger standing on the sidewalk at our front gate. He must have been waiting for Justin. Why?

Where was this day heading? The likes of this man I had never before seen. From my angle he stood about five feet ten inches tall, his complexion medium brown, with an austere look on his face. He was not too skinny, yet not fat; there was, as some would say, 'meat on his bones,' under a light grey and pink striped tee.

Standing with his body slightly tilted towards the house, he faced somewhat forward. The creaking sound of the door opening and the 'click, clack' of my heels coming down the stairs must have reached his ears but he did not look up.

"Who was this stranger?" I wondered to myself. Almost immediately it dawned on me: It must be one of those drug pushers. Maybe he was waiting on Justin to come out with his money. Justin must have bought marijuana or some other drugs from him and did not pay him. Or could it have been that Justin was selling drugs for this man and did not give the man his money?

At the foot of the stairs I pretended not to notice the man, and neither did he look in my direction but maintained his position as I headed down the walkway.

The gate opened inward, and as he stood more to the side of the gate, I walked out without having to say excuse me or such the like. Whatever was taking place here certainly did not look good.

Thoughts flooded my mind: "Should I call Justin's grandfather on the phone and let him know that a drug pusher was out front waiting on his grandson? What if I called him and he came out and the man shot the grandfather then I would have to live with that. My goodness me!"

My husband was upstairs getting dressed to leave shortly; I thought it would be best to call him and warn him about the situation that was unfolding before my very eyes.

Walking ahead to the other block in the direction in which the man was looking, I was trying to see without turning my head what the man was up too. At the same time I called my husband on my cell phone.

Getting him up to speed on the goings on thus far and the fact that Justin had not yet returned to give the man his money, I urged him to exercise caution when opening the door to venture outside.

Neil's voice was calm as he assured me he would be okay. That seemed to quell my anxieties because the moment I hung up the phone I had forgotten about what just transpired.

Catching sight of the train station a few minutes away impressed upon me the need to quicken my pace. Just then the phone rang. It was Neil on the other end: "Girl, what's the matter with you? That was Daren outside waiting for me."

"Which Daren? You mean your friend, 'Chinee'?" I inquired.

"Yes," he replied. "Did you forget I told you he was coming to meet me? You didn't remember him? You met him before. He laughed when I told him you thought he was a drug pusher." Neil couldn't stop laughing himself.

"Wow! Why didn't he say hello to me or something? He did not even look in my direction. How would I know he was not a drug pusher? He looked so serious as if somebody owed him something. Ok, well at least we are all safe and sound and no one was shot. Well, as the saying goes, all's well that ends well. See you later. Love you much, bye." And with those parting words I hung up the phone and went my merry way.

Chapter Two

The two car party made their way through little villages. As we went past, often times you would see bare back, bare feet little boys, and bare feet little girls, playing in the all dirt yards, at the front of their homes.

Slowing down, as the road narrowed and meandered overlooking treacherous cliffs, we caught glimpses of naturally landscaped areas with their wide array of tree tops attempting to stretch upwards, as if to catch a view of the passersby.

Loud music bellowed from an approaching upstairs and downstairs, concrete house, and what seemed to be everyone and his neighbor were all gathered there on the front lawn.

The smoke from barbecue and the strong curry aroma blended together amidst the din of the folks laughing, talking and whatever else they were engaged in.

Get It Off Me

A quarrel seemed to have erupted at a card table a little further down. We could tell by the facial expressions, and the gestures of the man standing over the table looking somewhat unsteady on his feet. The blazing heat of the tropical sun almost certainly had nothing to do with that. No doubt, tempers flare easily when persons consume alcohol without restraint which, seemed to be the case.

Leaving the stretch of straight road completely behind, we were now driving through a narrow, two lane, meandering road with varying gradients.

As we drove along, window glass all the way down, faces drinking in the fresh, clean, tropical air, the side of the mountain was laid out on our right, and deep precipices to the left.

At many a sharp curve we honked our horn to alert oncoming vehicular traffic of our presence, so all involved would drive with caution.

Suddenly, the mountains dropped out of sight only to expose the marvelous beauty of the foamy blue waters below, away in the distance.

Everything bubbled inside as for me there were few things more magnificent. How breathtaking the creation that speaks volume of its awe inspiring creator who wisely set the "bars for the sea."

Too distant to actually hear the lapping of the waves on the sea shore, I imagined it: ever so soothing, oh, so delightful.

Two hours or so had gone by and having turned off to the right of the ever so winding road, and off the mountain into the valley, we proceeded down a fairly wide, paved road that lead onto somewhat of a stone strewn expanse, ahead of which, at last, in all reality, sat Manzanilla beach.

This little piece of the so called 'paradise isle' was surrounded by some coconut trees amidst others, the names of which I was clueless. Nonetheless, every tree and every bit of shrubbery lent itself to the ambience of the area that beckoned you to step in and enjoy.

A cold soft drink to refresh ourselves and then it was a sudden rush to get into bathing gear. There were no changing stalls so we took turns changing in the car with towels hung at the windows and a screen at the windscreen for privacy. Whenever someone was changing inside someone stood guard outside.

I was all changed into my cherished blue and white polka dot swim suit I had bought from Pat on her return from her last trip to England.

There I was, standing guard for the last female in the group to get out of her jeans and tee shirt into her bathing suit when, suddenly, a scream came from within the little bluish grey four door sedan. What could be wrong? She was all alone changing, and previously three of us had taken turns changing in there without incident.

Quickly spinning around, I opened the door just enough to ask, "Are you ok? What's the matter?"

Now she was really screaming without let up. She was writhing on the seat trying to come forward whilst holding onto the back of her red swim suit at the buttocks. I heard this horrible crunching sound coming from where she was holding. It sent chills down my spine. A look of sheer terror on her face as she pleaded with me, "Help me! Get it of me!"

She was trying to get out of the car whilst still holding onto the rear end of her swim wear. She screamed, "An insect is in my bathing suit."

Horrified, I opened the car door wide to help her get out, at the same time attempting to reassure her: "The guys will get it out; try not to wriggle too much so that whatever it is doesn't sting you."

By this time, the other friends had gathered around to render whatever assistance they could. She was now outside the car, still holding on to the beast that somehow got inside her bathing suit, apparently, as she was pulling it up.

From the sound of it, that was no little beast. It must have been something with a hard, crusty outer shell... oh yuck!

"Please help me; get it off me!" was her agonized plea, tears rolling down her cheeks. As terrified as I was of insects I felt her distress.

One of the young men told her: "Let go of it, I will hold

Get It Off Me

it whilst one of these brave ladies reach in and take it out." I encouraged her to stay calm so operation 'remove the insect' could take place.

As she calmed down somewhat, and moved her hand away, the young man grabbed onto it; the creckling sound amplified from the crushing strength of a more powerful hold. Quickly, another young man reached in, way down inside the back of her swimsuit, and wrenched the beast out. All of us ladies were chickens.

"Eeeeee," was the sound she made, whilst he was pulling it out, trying to stay still and not scream. With a swift pitch he threw the supposed critter down.

"What is it?" she asked as it fell with a thud to the ground.

It did not look at all as what we would have expected; it was in a crumpled white plastic bag. How did the beast get in the bag and get in the car?

One of the ladies said: "Someone must have brought that insect with them, unknowingly, in their bag. For sure, by now it must be dead after what it just went through. Open it and see!"

And so the young man picked up the bag and opened it. Afraid the supposed beast would jump out, I quickly stepped back thinking for sure it would be gross looking.

We were all in for a major surprise as the young man exclaimed: "No, I can't believe this; are you serious? Tamarind?* ...who would do this?"

He reached in the bag and pulled out his hand; with palm opened, there laid upon it, three sticks of tamarind; their shells all cracked up from all the wriggling and crushing heaped upon them; everyone busted out laughing.

"My tamarind, oh man!" I blurted out. "I am so, so, sorry. I completely forgot; I had put those for me to eat while we were driving up here. Oh man, I forgot. Please forgive me," I offered. They all stared at me in amazement and laughed.

Then the girl who was attacked by my tamarind said: "You and your tamarind... well, let's do what we came here to do, let's go enjoy the beautiful sea."

With that we all made a mad dash, running on to the sand, and into the invigorating warm water of the sea at Manzanilla.

Feel free to take a dip if ever you visit Trinidad and Tobago. Please, just be sure, on your way there, to eat your tamarind - sweet or sour, and avoid the drama.

* What you may not know .....Page 98

Was Not Lost but Was
FOUND

Chapter Three

It may have been just another Saturday, but to almost every school child, that represented the ever so looked forward to weekly break away from school. For me it was no different.
Having sauntered down the road mostly for the fun of it, I took a right turn off Prince Street onto Broadway.
Busy, busy, busy; that little stretch of shopping area thrived with the usual hum of shoppers going to and fro, and a few pavement vendors trying to get you to buy their wares.
The warmed air, thick with the aroma of fried chicken, seemed to trail me as I went past the chicken and chips fast food outlet on my way to the craft store. In less than a minute, the door to the dimly lit store stood within a

Was Not Lost

hand's breath. No air condition, no windows, just the opened front door allowed entry of the warm breeze.

Stepping into Madame Chapeau's store brought one face to face with shelved walls, filled with various craft items; most of which seemed unidentifiable inside their protective plastic bags.

Inside the door on my right, the tall glass show case stood like king amongst others of various height and width that occupied the majority of the floor space. They housed the more delicate items for sale in the store.

To be sure, Madame Chapeau, the proprietor and sole salesperson, knew what was in every package and its exact location. Whatever your requested item, if it was in her inventory, she would immediately retrieve it either from the packed shelves or one of the glass showcases.

It seemed more than likely that Madame Chapeau's store was filled with items sure to meet the needs of most of the customers who flowed in and out.

As one of those customers, I was enticed by some hair ornaments and crochet thread; so with them in hand, away to the cashier for me, and then to head my merry way home.

I had dipped my hand in my pocket, to get my money to pay, when, to my surprise, I pulled out a twenty dollar bill. "Oooh...!" Amazed and excited, thoughts raced around in my head; attempting to pinpoint when and where I had put that cash in my pants pocket.

After a few minutes of deliberation, the brain concluded: "I had forgotten that I had this, maybe it was money I thought I had lost." In fact, the brain caused a major pleasant feeling to course through my being.

It was mightily invigorating from my brain's standpoint to realize that maybe I had been disciplined enough to have saved this, notwithstanding the fact that I knew not when or how I got it; but man, oh man, I was certainly delighted to have found it.

At this point the best thing to do was to pretend it never existed and put it in the bank. Could it have been that my thoughts were veering towards entrepreneurship? Are those not the folks who say: "....money saved is money earned?" So the five dollars that I knowingly came with to spend was just what I used to pay for my items, collected my change, and headed home.

Banks were closed on Saturdays so I had to wait until Monday to put my twenty dollar bill into my account.

It occurred to me, strange as it seemed, that I had not encountered any school friends when I went shopping or running errands. Neither on my way home did I encounter any of them.

Maybe I had no friends except Kate and April two of my neighbors. They were not in my class and I don't remember if they even went to my school. Well, I think April did but I'm not one hundred percent sure....

Anyway, next up was Tantie* Priscilla's shop. It was just before my home and, as always, it was the place where almost everyone en route stopped to buy a snack or two before heading in.

The glass showcase that sat on top the counter, laid bare all the goods, for sale, that Tantie Priscilla had made herself: sugar cake*, the infamous tamarind balls*, fudge of varying kinds, and other local treats and sweets.

Displayed on the shelved wall facing the customer were jars filled with other goodies for purchase: sweet and salt prunes, salt prunes, red mango (with and without pepper), and spicy red plums, among others.

For me it was the absolute same; I had to pick up a snack before heading in; nothing better than a mars bar to chew on once inside. As for tamarind balls, I made my own, by the dozens...uuhhmm.

Last stop, thirty two Prince Street, my place of residence, my mini castle, where Tantie Vio almost spoiled me rotten (please don't spoil your kids or grandkids or anyone for that matter - no good). The six red stairs were no match for me as I ran up two at a time.

Excitedly, I showed Tantie Vio my purchased goods. The lily white crochet thread was for me to make a tie. She had taught me to crochet from the age of seven and she was proud of my progress.

"Very good," she said "now where are my things I sent you to get?"

Was Not Lost

"Your things?" I asked inquiringly, "what things?"

Tantie Vio almost jumped out of her skin, her light brown face coming down to meet mines, her eyes, opened wide staring at me as she blurted out: "Little girl, don't play with me. Where is my twenty dollars I gave you? I asked you to go out for me. You weren't going anywhere; I sent you on an errand. Now you come here showing me things you bought. I hope you didn't spend my twenty dollars....or else...girl...."

"Oooooooooohhhhh!" I exclaimed, "That was your twenty dollars! OOhoo! I forgot; I have it; I have it. Don't get mad; I'll go back and buy what you need. Let me write it down."

So I had no money to put in the bank on Monday because it was not my 'was lost now it's found money,' it was Tantie Vio's money. Wow! Just as well the banks were closed. At least I had some good business sense which sure saved me added stress.

* What you may not know .....Page 98

Chapter Four

The Eastern Main Road, crammed packed with after school traffic in eighty five degree Fahrenheit temperature, made the journey seem like sixty miles. My cherished white banded, quartz watch showed the time to be 4.30 pm.

The bus had left the terminal over an hour and a half ago, yet had travelled no further than a few miles of the sixteen mile trip from Port-of-Spain in the West to Arima in the East. Mostly school children, teenagers, filled the bus, seated and standing. Hardly was there room for a fly.

Some were attempting to do homework, while others talked about anything, and some chattered about nothing. There were never any fights on the bus, and no one ever seemed to fall out with anyone, at least, if they did, I never heard about it.

Everybody knew that this boy from St Mary's College

and this girl from Bishop Anstey High school were dating. They travelled together every day and were always very quiet. They were older and finished high school before I did and heard they got married right after they graduated.

I was not privileged to get a seat right away, so every time the bus stopped to drop someone off, I looked around for my chance to a vacated one.

Caroline stood next to me with her left hand stretched upward, holding onto the rail, whilst her right hand held on to the crook of the left. With this support, she placed her head quite comfortably on her outstretched arm and, was sound asleep. Unlike me, she was not trying to find a seat; she was away to slumber land.

The bumping and jerking of the bus on the often times pot-hole riddled, paved road never seemed to jar her out of her beauty nap; well, for the length of time we were on the bus that was no nap, the girl was plain 'ole' sleeping. Now and again she would let out a little snore. No one seemed to pay her any mind, and she would not have been in the least bit concerned even if they did, before she went to sleep, or after she awoke.

She was smart. After all she was a Bishops' girl... (some folks thought that was a big deal....just so you know); she attended Bishop Anstey High School, it was supposed to be prestigious.

I should have learned a lesson or two from her: get some shut eye on the bus, so when you get home late, around five-thirty or six in the evening, which was more often than not the case, you would not feel so sleep deprived.

For me, getting home at those hours meant staying up late to do homework. But generally the bus was fun so I enjoyed that.

Three stops before mine, the two passengers seated where I was standing got out, so without hesitation, I slid right in and sat and rested my weary legs. With the bus now relieved of the majority of passengers, it provided me the ability to set my heavy bag down on the empty seat next to me, much to my relief.

We sometimes had debates on one topic or another.

Bags Of Books

We were just in the heart of our discussion when the bus pulled into its final stop just after the dial* in Arima. As if orchestrated, when the bus came to a halt so did the discussion. Yes, nobody attempted to finish even a sentence at those times. We were all trying to get off the bus and get home.

And that's where I headed in one of my frequently glad moods. I had only walked a few feet away from the bus when I heard a man's serious sounding voice from behind me.

"Hello, hello, little miss...."

Scarcely was there time to think when a heavy hand tapped my right shoulder. Startled, I swiftly turned around and came face to face with the bus conductor standing just a tad taller than my five feet, three inches. His round face was as serious as a judge as he stared me down with semi squinting eyes.

"Obviously, you did not go to school today. What is going on with you?" He asked, but before I could respond he continued: "Where is your school bag? Did you take a bag of books with you to school today?" He all but got out a belt to beat me.

"I went to school; oh, my bag, I forgot my bag of books. I forgot my book bag." I managed to get out pitifully, looking at my bag in his hand. What could I say? Dumfounded, I just looked at him and said, "I was talking and forgot it." With outstretched arm reaching for my bag, I said, "Thank you sir."

"Thank you? Thank you?" he retorted. "I know your father and I'm going to talk to him about you. No child who went to school, or is interested in school would walk off and leave their bag of books on the bus."

He handed me the bag and said: "Go on! And you had better go straight home!"

Under his breath he muttered, "Wayward!"

If only he knew, the thought of skipping school never crossed my mind; and even if it did, I might have forgotten Oh well! Homeward bound, I merrily continued my journey.

If my father had heard of this he would not have been

surprised. He had always said that I should be grateful to God for the provision of a neck. According to him, if my head was not attached to my body via my neck I would have been walking around like a headless chicken. He figured I would have put my head down somewhere, forgotten to pick it up, then not remember where that somewhere was....imagine that!

Tidbit: Well, we should all be grateful for our necks- we don't have to turn our whole body to look around. In addition, the neck may appear simple but it is a rather complex part of the human anatomy, with portions of not only skeletal, but also muscular, glandular and digestive system, housed within this little framework that we so often take for granted.

This must be part of what King David was thinking about when he said to his creator in the holy writings: "I shall laud you because in a fear-inspiring way I am wonderfully made." Truly, if you do some research on the neck, you too will have the same conclusion: wonderful, absolutely wonderful!

Chapter Five

Sprinting from the sofa I headed into the kitchen, remembering, that in an effort to get an early start the next day, some advanced preparation for breakfast and lunch was necessary.

'Slower than molasses in winter,' was not an over exaggeration on my account. Many a friend and family called it 'titivating;'* you could say, like a hamster on a treadmill, constantly moving but going nowhere. It was often said that for every step I took forward, I took two backwards.

Truthfully, cooking to me was a chore unless we were having company. Begging my heavenly father to help me love my family enough to want to, and to enjoy cooking for them, was an almost daily petition.

People who love to cook always cook tasty meals. I needed to put some love in my cooking to tastefully feed

Three Strips

the people I love the most.

Many a times I had forgotten I needed to cook dinner until maybe around four in the afternoon when I realized: "Oops! They'll be home soon and I haven't started anything just yet." To keep from screaming meant supplication to God for help to maintain my composure while running the frustrated marathon to get dinner ready; it worked every time. Bless Jah!

Now ready to get up to speed to bring tomorrow's meals to fruition, I looked to my little cherished, pine wood, kitchen table; always ready to handle the work load. But wait! How odd; something upon my precious table brought me to a screeching halt.

It was puzzling to see lying there on the table, absent of anything else but my cute, little, black vase with the sugar flower bulbs Akeyla had made for her wedding cake, was a clear, plastic, freezer bag.

Lying inside the bag was some white paper towel; three strips of select-a-size paper towel to be exact. Oddly, the strips were not separated. What in the world was this doing there? Where would that have come from? Who would have put it there?

Analyzing the situation, and trying to put the pieces of the puzzle together, I ran through the various scenarios in my mind. Could it be that this was a bag Neil had used to put his fruits in to take to work? Hardly likely; we used one strip of paper towel per washed fruit. Had it been the regular size paper towel sheet, which we very seldom purchased, then it would have been two fruits per sheet. So that was immediately ruled out sending me on a frenzied hunt for an answer.

I asked our guest if she was responsible for putting the plastic freezer bag on the table, and that met with a definitive, "No."

There were only three of us in the apartment; I knew for sure it was not Neil. I asked her again; maybe she had forgotten that she had put it there, but still she denied knowing anything about it.

"Just throw the bag out," she told me.

After hearing my dilemma, Neil echoed the exact

sentiment.

"Are you guys crazy?" I asked. "I have to find out where this bag came from and why it is on my table. I have no idea whether it's clean or dirty and I need to know. I can't throw it out until I know for sure where it came from."

Who would do such a thing? Why would they put this bag on my table? They kept insisting that I throw the bag in the garbage. Were they hard of hearing? Did they not hear me say that I could not throw it out until I found out its origin?

It was imperative for my peace of mind to find out what was initially housed in that bag, and exactly where it came from? Not having those answers were frustrating the daylights out of me. So in an effort to get to solve this case, the process of elimination continued.

Maybe it was our house guest's husband. She was staying with us for a while as they were having some work done in their apartment. They were wonderful, close friends, more like family. The husband would come over and we would have dinner together some evenings.

He was over last evening. Maybe he had brought the bag and left it on the table and it had escaped my notice. Although nothing in my apartment escaped my notice, I was willing to accept that as the only plausible reason for that bag being where it was.

We were not in the habit of taking out three strips of paper towel at the same time. Two strips when drying a dish, but not three.

Anxiously we awaited, well, I awaited the arrival of the husband that evening.

Those other two adults with me couldn't care less, as they kept on harping on the fact that I should just throw the bag out and finish with it. It could never be finished with until there was an explanation. I needed closure!

No sooner had the husband entered the apartment than I accosted him to get to the bottom of this conundrum. Taking him into the kitchen I showed him the mystery bag lying on the table. To my utter dismay he denied knowing anything about it.

Three Strips

Really, now I wanted to scream. This was becoming more of a horrifying mystery by the minute.

Somebody had to be responsible for putting that bag there. It had no arms, and no legs, so it could not have climbed up and sat there on its own. Somebody had to put those three strips inside it and set it down there.

To quell my spirit, I decided it was best to go about my preparation but left the bag on the table until this could be straightened out. Things had become more complex than I would have ever imagined.

I finished what I needed to take care of, and having used the chopped pumpkin, the freezer bag that held it was now empty. With freezer bag in hand I proceeded to go to the kitchen sink and wash it out with dish detergent and water. 'Critical times hard to deal with' (according to the second book of Timothy, chapter two verse one) were upon us, so I did my part not only to save the environment but also to preserve our pockets.

Whenever the bags were washed, I would not let them drip dry, for fear some insect may have flown into or crawled around in the bag without my knowledge. My preference had been to dry the bag instantly or else I would have been forced to throw it out. I would then reuse the paper towel to wipe areas in the bathroom before disposal; reuse to reduce...makes 'cents'.

This time was no different. Reaching for the paper towel I pulled out three strips and proceeded to dry the bag....I gasped: "Oh dear! It was me all along. So I was the one who put the three strips of paper towel in the bag."

It all came back to me. I was in the process of drying the bag with the three strips of paper towel when the phone rang; immediately putting the bag on the table I went to answer the phone, then sat on the sofa and chatted with my friend for quite a 'lil' while, with many a laughter in between, and completely forgot about the task with which I was previously engaged.

Finally, the mystery was solved; yes, the three persons in the apartment me, myself and I were responsible for putting that bag on my table. Searching feverishly and fervently for the culprit was the culprit herself. How crazy was that? My apologies were accepted amidst all their laughter at my crazy self. If you laugh too, then it is all good.   If you know what causes problems like that, pleeeaaase tell me.

*What you may not know.....Page 98

Chapter Six

The tiny, tropical, twin island republic of Trinidad and Tobago, most southerly in location in the Caribbean, was as good a place as any to grow up, go to school, and make friends.

There, at Arima Girls' RC School, was the place where my earliest friendships would or should have been formed. The building sat just a tad over a five minute walk from where we lived on Prince Street, in the small town of Arima, in the eastern quadrant of the island.

Four adults and one child occupied that residence. The house sat on two plots of land, 'plop' in the middle, with that parcel of land located at a corner of the street.

The three bedroom place called home to us at 32 Prince Street was a split level house without a split. The front of the building sat low on the ground but the back was high of the ground.

For me, running up the six permanently painted red stairs to the front of the house, was always a breeze; the twenty five concrete, unpainted stairs at the back

No Friends

prompted a more cautious ascent or descent as there were no protective railings.

It was there my friends would visit with me. Then again, what friends? There was one girl Debbie we were friends at school and we walked home together but then she migrated to the United States of America and I never saw or heard from her again. Maybe she's on a social network site... if ever I remember to check....who knows? .

To be sure, there are things you must do in order to make friends and retain them. Absolutely essential is that one must first be the friend that you want others to be; maybe those elements were lacking in my character.

Ah, sadly, that could have been the result of overindulgence heaped upon me by my overly beloved Tantie Vio. ("Do not spoil your children please. It's not healthy for them or you. There is a real, sometimes cruel world out there. Help them to thrive in spite of it.")

Interestingly, the apparent lack of friends during those years never seemed to have affected me. It must have been that Tantie Vio's adult company and the bonding that happened with my four older siblings, whenever I visited my parents' home, were sufficient.

Remember what has been said about reaping? What have I sown? Whatever has been heaped upon me has been earned for what I did to three girls who came home with me one evening from school.

They were granted a special privilege to see a prized possession that I had supposedly received from abroad. It was so precious that they had to promise not to tell anyone about it.

The names of the girls, or what they looked like, have been erased from my memory; but certainly they were the most compliant bunch one had ever encountered. They were ordered not to repeat what they saw to anyone; not even to each other. According to my warnings, to repeat what they saw would definitely have put them in harm's way. Oh boy!

Obediently, they all gathered in my gallery (porch), and one by one, were taken into the front bedroom to see this precious possession.

The one always known just as an extremely talkative child; the 'good worker but much too talkative' child, according to my teachers, was now displaying a side unknown to all, and even to me.

The truthfulness of these words from the holy writings became apparent: "Wickedness is tied up in the heart of a boy (girl)."

Inside that front room, one by one they were brought in as "sheep to the slaughter;" not having a clue as to what lay ahead. Each girl in turn was told she could not scream or make any sound and, to close the eyes until told to open them.

With a strange kind of obedience, and completely trusting, each obliged as a bottle was put under the nose and then the order went out into their ear, "Take a deep breath with your mouth closed." The poor trusting child pulled up through the nostril only to let out a scream which was quickly covered with my free hand.

The sudden pull and the resultant rush of the gas up the nasal cavity caused the eyes to shoot open with the accompanying scream. Cruel, cruel, cruel!!! Yes, it was a bottle of smelling salts; the so called 'precious possession' that they were gullibly led to inhale. To think that was the scheme of an eight year old child. Sadly, there is a lesson here for all parents: "Train your children to not visit their friends' homes at these tender ages unsupervised."

Never was I allowed to visit any one's home without an adult. Tantie Vio must have been downstairs washing or she would not have allowed this. In any event they never visited me again. In spite of the warning they must have spread the word about that rather awful act.

No wonder, and quite deserving, I had no friends visit my home for quite a long, long time. To those girls and their parents: "If ever you read this book, please know that sincerely, I apologize, I truly am sorry."

NOTE TO PARENTS: The world today is much worse than smelling salts....protect your children, please.

Chapter Seven

In spite of the doctors best efforts, conventional medication regimens were proving futile. Neil's high blood pressure refused to budge. He had already given up smoking years ago when we were pregnant with our son and first child, Yohance; he was also not given to heavy drinking.

His diagnosis of high blood pressure came at the time when he had been hospitalized because of a broken left tibia. An opponent had landed such a kick on his lower left leg during a football (soccer) match that it broke, sending the jagged edge of the broken bone right through the skin just above the ankle.

After many painful hours in the emergency room at the Port-of-Spain General Hospital, he was finally wheeled into the operating theatre. Had it not been for the compassion of a doctor who had taken notice of him, there

Belching Smoke

was no telling what time he would have been attended too; and what negative consequences he could have faced from the delayed treatment.

He had been on a stretcher for hours without having been examined; the doctor remembered seeing him there earlier on into his shift. He could not believe that there he was, about to go off duty, and that patient had not yet been seen. Immediately he got things moving.

The cause of his hypertension, whether stress from the accident, or genetics, or other factors, was never determined; but it was something that this nineteen year old had to contend with for the rest of his life.

For a while it seemed manageable; and by the time we got married we had all but forgotten about it; at least I did.

Forgotten, but not gone. It surely in time rose its ugly head; so we tried to slay it by cutting down on salt. By age thirty it had taken full control so the battle to take his life back was on.

Notwithstanding the human desire to satisfy the taste buds, we really had to put up a hard fight. It was this war that put him in the firing line.

The firing line from anyone, and everyone, who used any herb, leaf or bush for themselves, or their cousin, aunt, mother's sister or father's brother for high blood pressure and got any kind of results real or imagined. Whether they boiled it, baked it, dried it, it did not matter. A desperate soul will try anything. And so it was that he really tried.

Here came the leaves of a certain tree that someone told him was guaranteed to reduce his blood pressure. Oh boy! He almost stripped the tree bare; every time he passed he took a bunch of leaves and not a small bunch at that.

Poor tree! For sure, it must somehow have been able to produce leaves at an extraordinarily rapid rate to keep up with the pace at which he removed them.

He would boil the leaves and let them sit for a few hours, then he would drink that water several times a day. It was those leaves that almost got us into a very dangerous situation. Those leaves? Yes, those leaves.

It was another working day for him and he was all set to head out; but instead of going to the front door he turned towards the kitchen. Why? Did he forget his lunch? No he did not. After finding out why, I gently turned him in the other direction, ushered him to the door, kissed him, closed the door behind him, turned the key in the lock, and headed to the kitchen.

At the entrance of the kitchen, I reached up and turned off the light switch, and with that made a roundabout turn and went into my bedroom.

Sighing with appreciative relief of being able to get back into bed I reached for my alarm clock, set it to wake me in another hour and in a blink, fell right back into slumber land.

I thought I was dreaming when I heard, "Mummy, mummy," as I felt a little hand waking me.

"Smoke is bothering me. Smoke is bothering me in my room." It was my four year old daughter Akeyla rousing me from sleep.

"Oh my goodness, who would be burning trash this hour of the morning? These neighbors have absolutely no consideration. That is so ridiculous! Come here in my bed and sleep." At least this way we could both go back to sleep; or so I thought.

I should have known that my little girl, once awakened in the morning, would not let that happen. She was bright eyed and bushy tailed and wanted her precious stomach satisfied. Her ritual had been, and that day was no different, "Mummy I'm hungry, mummy I'm hungry," and "mummy, I'm hungry."

This repetitive acknowledgement of her state of being hungry, continued on and on, with only a brief pause just long enough for me to plead with her to go back to sleep.

"Keel, mummy will die if she has to get out of bed right now."

"Mummy, I'm hungry, mummy I'm hungry, mummy I'm hungry," was her response; obviously oblivious to my death plea; or maybe her recognition of the nonsensical nature of that overly dramatic statement. In her intelligent little mind, that required no acknowledgement; so she

Belching Smoke

persisted in her effort to satisfy her more pressing need to be fed.

My offer to pray with her was eagerly accepted. Then being very, very unwilling mentally and physically to drag myself out of bed, I read her a story from the beautifully illustrated, "My Book of Bible Stories" published by Watchtower Bible and Tract Society, which she always enjoyed.

Relentlessly, the words drummed into my ears. Again and again, like a stuck record, it finally got to me. Dragging out of bed I acquiesced and proceeded to fulfill her desire. With that I headed into the kitchen only to see thick smoke belching out of the arched doorway.

"What in the world is this?" I thought out loud.

Bewildered I tried clearing the smoke with my right hand while pulling up my pajama top to cover my nose and mouth to prevent choking as I headed into the kitchen. Mumbling, I sought to understand the culprit behind this smoke.

"I don't cook this early so why is there smoke in my kitchen?" Barely had those words escaped my lips when it hit me like a thunderbolt as I saw the pot of fire on the stove.

Neil had put some of those leaves to boil before he left. He was heading to the kitchen to turn of the stove when I assured him that I would turn it off.

He had a troubled look on his face when he said, "You know how you forget stuff; please make sure to turn off the stove right away. Don't go to sleep with the stove on."

Assuredly, my bold face response? "I am up; of course I won't leave the stove on. After you leave I'll go and turn it off." Can you imagine having had that discussion and then in one split second you do something totally opposite? It was as if when I turned the lock on the front door after him that something turned off in my brain

Hurriedly I opened the back door, turned off the stove grabbed the pot with a pot holder, threw it outside then doused it with water.

The moment of truth had admittedly arrived: I needed help. Something was dreadfully wrong with my brain.

How would one react to something like that?

And now, just around four o'clock in the afternoon, the dreaded time of reckoning came. The front gate was opened and the 'clang' of it being closed seemed to reverberate throughout the apartment. In about thirty seconds that was followed by the sound of the turning of a key, the 'crecking' of the wrought iron outer gate being opened, then the unlocking of the front door; it was him.

In a hurried dash I ran towards Neil as he stepped inside, and without saying a greeting to him, I sternly but gently ordered him to not say a word and don't get upset.

"Just get me help," I blurted out rapidly. "Obviously I need help. It seemed as if when I turned the key in the lock behind you this morning that something must have switched off in my brain. I walked to the kitchen and completely forgot about the stove; I turned out the light and went back to bed."

Once again I expressed, "I need help."

Strangely enough, he seemed stuck for words as the entire ordeal was recounted to him. He too must have recognized our dilemma and maybe, silently, wondered what in the world he had got himself into the day he said "I do."

"Huh," seemed to be all he could have mustered up and with a seemingly baffled shake of his head, continued into the house and went about his evening as usual.

And so, I too continued my day as most others; and that was that....

Chapter Eight

Finishing off business in the city early and being ready to head home felt good. It was still rush hour; but for me that was an early hour. Neil would be getting off work just about now so it would be good to pick him up. That would be a welcome surprise, both of us being able to get home together; a rare treat for us and for the kids as well.

Amidst the crowded streets and the inevitable traffic jam, we graciously made our way up the eastern main road. The drive home, although only about twelve miles, would take the better part of two hours.

The alternate route along the highway on the east west corridor was probably no better, being heavily weighted with traffic at that time as well.

In any event, we would still need to get back to the

Chinese

eastern main road which meant driving along a connecting secondary road from west to east. All of these secondary roads at peak time were also well crammed since everyone seemed to have the same idea: to get to their destination faster. It was nothing but a mind game; fooling oneself into thinking that one route was faster than the other.

Along the eastern main road there were diverse sights and sounds that lent themselves to an interesting commute as traffic crawled up the road on what was a gorgeous day.

Mild tropical breezes wafted through the air bringing with it the tantalizing scents of local cuisine from the many and varied restaurants, local shops, and homes along the way.

"Do you have food at home for me?" Neil suddenly asked. The distinctive aroma of delicious food must have started his mouth watering.

"I was thinking of getting Chinese food for dinner," He added as we were passing one of our favorite Chinese restaurants.

That was very strange I thought. Then I asked in wonderment, "Why would there not be food for you? We have never eaten and left you without food have we?"

I was really taken aback by that. Why would he even have thought as such?

"Or, okay, you are right, I guess 'Chinese' was on my mind," he said as we continued our journey.

We had gone no more than five minutes when my heart fluttered as I was brought back to earth; how would you have food for him when you did not even cook?

Immediately I blurted out: "Why don't we buy the Chinese food and take home for dinner. That would be a nice surprise for the kids."

Huh! Can you imagine getting home, hungry after a hard day's work, expecting a nice hot meal, only to find out that there was nothing to eat? Worse yet, to think that you had been assured that, yes, dinner would be served but really dinner had not even been cooked. Who does that???

With joy in my heart over the fact that he had made the suggestion of getting Chinese food, I happily turned the car around all but whistling with excitement as we headed back to the restaurant to purchase our dinner. My husband saved the day and he did not even know it. Wheeeww!

Chapter Nine

"Did you pay the light bill?" Neil asked as we approached the darkened apartment around 7.30 one evening.

"Me? You are the one who pays the light bill. Did you pay the light bill?" I retorted as he turned into the driveway.

The 'Sccrruuunnncch' of the tires on the graveled ground was interrupted by the neighbor calling out to me urgently as she approached the car: "Donna, Donna, the lady was here several times with Yohance but nobody was here to get him."

"Where is Jackie?" I inquired.

"I don't know. There was no one here," She replied.

"That is not like Jackie," I began, when Neil interrupted with the words: "Get in the car! Let's go! You're always hiring these people to work and you can't

Keys

rely on them. I don't know where you find them." He was obviously angry as he reversed onto the street and headed up the road to Jackie's home.

"You know Jackie is not like that. Jackie is very responsible. She is always on time and she has never disappointed us so don't say things like that. There has to be a logical explanation for this," was the best I could offer in return.

Baffled as we drove over to her home, I struggled to figure out what could have caused Jackie to not show up for work without informing me. She was always reliable, punctual. In fact she was nothing short of a dream; she made it so easy for me to run my business. The apartment she kept in tip top shape. She made all the necessary preparation for the kids when they came in from school. She knew what her responsibilities were and she carried them out extremely well.

In fact, she went above and beyond the call of duty. Just a telephone call to let her know that I was coming to get Yohance to take him for a run with me, as I did a product delivery or fulfilled an appointment with a prospect, got her into action.

Yohance would be showered and dressed and a snack bag packed by the time of my arrival. Never mind that would most likely have been his second shower since he was showered every morning. Jackie would make the run with us. Then we would get Akeyla when her school was over and continued our running around with Akeyla doing homework in the car. Jackie always had a snack packed for her too, and some bottles of water for all of us.

Yohance loved nothing better as he had 'gas brains' (he loved to ride in a vehicle all the time and did not care to walk anywhere) from very young. He got mad, when we were out driving, if we got stuck at a traffic light for too long.

My routine before heading into the city or wherever else business would take me, was to drop off the keys for Jackie; then sometime before 1.00 pm she would go over to the apartment. She would straighten things up around the home and care for the kids when they returned from school. She lived within the territory so we were just fifteen minutes walking distance apart.

So it was within minutes that her gate came into vision; and simultaneously, I gasped, mentally unable to comprehend the madness.

We were now in front her home. She must have seen us pulling up for she sauntered out strolling down her walkway towards us with a big grin on her face.

Before I could say a word Jackie asked in her loud cheerful voice: "Girl, what happened to you this morning? You did not bring the keys so I said: 'like Donna stayed home today'."

"Oh, my, word, I did not bring the keys!" That is exactly what I realized as we caught sight of Jackie's home.

Before I could say another word there was Neil calling to me again, "Get in the car!"

No sooner was I seated that he sternly charged: "So my son is still in school because you did not drop off the keys? Where is my daughter?" Understandably he was livid.

"People don't know what I have to go through," he continued.

"I could never feel comfortable at work. I never know if I'm going to come home one day and find my children burnt in the house because you forgot something on the stove." His voice dropped, almost to a whisper, considering the gravity of the situation, probably envisioning what could easily have been an even worse scenario.

"Where is Akeyla?" He asked.

"She must be over at Lisa's because that's the arrangement: if ever for any reason no one is home when she comes from school that's where she would go."

In no more than ten minutes we were at Yohance's school. I got out and walked into the building. There they were; Joy, the principal, with three of the teachers waiting patiently.

Yohance, unable to verbalize, creased his brow, fretted loudly, and grabbed my hand pulling me to go. I apologized profusely to all.

Thankfully, they were all very kind and understanding.

Keys

Joy had tried to get in touch with me but to no avail. She did not want to distress Neil by calling him on the job. She said she knew I would show up; they had made three trips to the house to drop him off but of course no one was there to receive him.

Their patience with me was remarkable. They must have known that something in my head did not fully compute.

Yohance and I headed back to the car with him still fretting with me in his own way.

Driving up our street in silence, we stopped four houses before ours on the opposite side to pick up Keyla from at Lisa's.

Akeyla was calm; not seeming in the least bit disturbed at our extreme tardiness. Not even batting an eye or asking why no one was at home when she got in from school. But that's Keyla for you; taking everything in stride. Such a gem! Years ago, when she was just a little over two years old, Neil said it well: "Akeyla is a real blessing from Jehovah."

Of course when we were all fed and showered no one needed to be prodded to go to bed. After a mentally exhausting evening, sleep so welcomed, did not come too soon.

Something to think about before we judge persons harshly: could it be, that sometimes, when a woman forgets her child in the car or somewhere else, could it just be that she has what I have? What is it? I can't say, but it may not necessarily be a negligent mother. Could it be an extremely forgetful mother? Probably she needs the help that I never realized or forgot to mention I needed. Help her please!

Chapter Ten

No two human beings are alike; and we all know that. Some persons have an overactive imagination but what accounts for that is beyond me.

Admittedly, there are those folks who are negative about most things in life. But just what do you call it when a person is almost always in a good mood, more often than not feels 'glad' even without money, and without drugs as props; yet, on the other hand, imagines the worst or weirdest scenarios out of life's ordinary situations?

Let's take a look at one such situation and you tell us what you think. Maybe, just maybe, you would have it figured out and able to provide an explanation; or maybe, it might very well remind you of you....

We had just moved into a new apartment. Well, not actually moved in because none of our possessions had been transferred there except Akeyla's burnt orange,

Cleopatra, sofa bed. This had just been purchased brand, spanking new from the store. The delivery guys had set it up that evening; and it surely lent itself to the flavor she wanted to bring to her space. She had that artsy flair.

Newly renovated, the apartment was outfitted with a nicely lacquered, somewhat l-shaped, wooden staircase that led into a small living room and a tiny kitchen. And I mean 'tiiinnny' kitchen. Strangely, I hadn't realized how 'chinkee'* the kitchen was when I first took the apartment. Nonetheless the ambience was quite remarkable.

The larger bedroom had his and hers walk-in-closet. The sunroof in the hallway and the height of the ceiling lightened the area and made it look roomier. It was great too that the hallway closet had quite a bit of storage space. Next to that closet was the very small bedroom where Akeyla's bed was placed.

What the apartment lacked in space it made up for in appeal. Through one of the windows in the living room you could step out onto a little patio out back that afforded us the awesome view of the sky. In fact, it became the hub for my daughter and her friends to hang out whenever they were over during the summer and fall.

And what do you know? Yes, the grown-ups were drawn to it too; my husband and his friends found that to be their go to spot.

Akeyla's family and friends photo table was both a tool and an entertainment piece designed just for that patio. Almost every visitor looked for their face somewhere on that table. Sadly it did not move with us to our next destination.

Yes, we moved several times. Someone tried to break in which prompted our move that time; we thought that it might have been an inside job. Need moving tips? You could check us out....should provide that service, right?

The apartment was clean but you never know who cleaned where, how, and with what; so Akeyla decided to spend the night there with me as I sanitized the entire apartment. Sanitizing wipes, bleach, LDC and some rolls of paper towel were some of the essentials I had brought along to tackle the job at hand.

Casing

Starting with the kitchen cabinets, I wiped every square inch of the interior and exterior before tackling the appliances, the window and door handles, etcetera. Taking a breather I headed for the main bedroom that was to be ours. For some strange reason I decided to take a peek out the front window. The view was nothing grand.

Just across the street was a school but that did not matter to us when we got the place. We weren't in that kind of income bracket, and neither did we have that kind of mind set, where people wanted this or that exclusive view. No, we just wanted a decent, affordable apartment in a reasonably safe neighborhood. Its location was ideal: close to the J and A train; the B38 and B15 bus lines both ran one block over, one on the east and the other to the south of us.

In spite of the school's proximity to us, the street was very quiet and clean. The back of the school compound is what faced us and generally there was very little if any activity there; we were very familiar with that area. The kids came in and exited at the front of the building on the other street to the north, Malcolm X.

No wonder, to me it was such a strange thing to see about four persons standing under the awning of the school building facing us. Looking up at the building, there were lights on, maybe they were having a night class. With that in mind I headed back to my cleaning.

Sometime later, I returned to the front room and decided to peek outside again; there were now about seven persons standing there across the street.

My curiosity now heightened I proceeded to look more intently at them and the surroundings hoping that they had not seen me. Why were they there? Why were they not moving? They were just standing there. At closer inspection I noticed it was drizzling slightly so it must have been that they were sheltering from the rain.

About ten minutes later there was no more rain but they had not moved; now my thoughts began racing, "Are they 'casing' the apartment?" I went into Akeyla's room, "Akeyla, wake up! I think there are people 'casing' the house; I think they want to rob us."

"Maaaa, we don't have anything in here for them to rob," was Akeyla's sleepy headed response.

She wasn't thinking straight and that's nothing new. It was always difficult to get through to her when she was dozing and worse yet when in deep slumber.

In an attempt to rouse her to action I continued in a low, but urgent tone: "Girl, they don't know that. All they know is that someone has moved into the apartment and maybe there are things that they can raid. They must be waiting for us to go to bed and then to make their move. We need to find a way to catch them in the process." Yes, we needed bait. My words were having little if any impact on Akeyla.

My suggestion was that we switch of the lights and flush them out as it were; then, as they began to make their move we would call the police and have them caught red handed. Akeyla thought that I was over the top and should just relax and forget about the people.

"Forget about the people? Yes, until they rob us or rather hurt us because we wasted their time since they could not get anything from us as we had nothing here for them to steal," I thought out loud.

Oh no! We have to be pro-active so with a flip of some switches we were in total darkness. Walking again to the front window and lifting a tiny end of the make shift sheet curtain I gasped in horror.

The group had moved away from the wall they were apparently leaning on and began moving, as if in slow motion, towards the house.

Running to Akeyla's room and shaking her out of sleep I whispered, "They are moving in; they are coming towards us; call the police! I'm going by the window to keep an eye on them; call the police, quick!"

Back at the window the group was now crossing the street and now their feet were hitting the sidewalk right in front of the house. With heart racing my soft call out to Akeyla that they are out front happened at the exact moment that a huge tour bus pulled up right in front of the group.

The driver got out and pulled down the side of the bus

Casing

and the people loaded luggage which for some reason I had not noticed before. They were going on some excursion or the other maybe Atlantic City, who knows? The driver closed the hatch and the folks then climbed onto the bus and off they went. What a thing! What a thing!

"Haha, hahaha, hahaha,"....... Akeyla could not stop laughing and I suppose you may be laughing now too.

*What you may not know.....Page 98

Chapter Eleven

How many times have you heard these words? "Hold on, I'll be right with you."
Rrrriiiiinnnng, rrring, rrring...... "Good day, Donna speaking, how may I help you?" Always expecting a customer on the other end of the line prompted my almost, always, professional response. This time it was my dear friend Yvonne.
"Aye girl, how are you doing?" Yvonne asked as the usual courtesy not really expecting a reply since we had just spoken about an hour ago. Practically without pausing she continued, "Girl, listen, I need you to tell me what you would recommend for someone with a yeast infection, also a man called me and he wanted a program for..." she was interrupted with a beep from my side of the phone.
"Hold on," I told her, "let me check this call; hold a second I'll be right back with you."
With those words, and a push of my index finger to

depress the button of the telephone, Yvonne's voice went off as she was put on hold and the call was switched to the caller on the other end.

"Good day, Donna speaking, how may I help you?"

"Hello Donna, I got your name from Glenda. She told me she orders these natural health products from you and that I may benefit from something for my...." The lady continued to explain her situation.

She had a host of health issues and wanted to get a nutrition support program that would be of benefit to her. I explained to her: "We do not offer a cure for anything but the products simply provide the body with the nutrients it requires in the balance the body requires it; then the body now has the necessary ammunition to look after itself."

She was helped to appreciate that we do not advise anyone to come off their prescribed medication.

I informed her: "Once you begin using the products, and the body continues to receive the needed quality nutrients, and as your health improves your doctor may see the need to reduce your medication, and as in many cases we have seen, they may eventually be able to wean you of medication altogether."

After several minutes of answering all her questions she was informed of the suggested nutrition support program for her particular challenge, along with the cost.

As with every customer, she was informed of the ability to get the products at a discounted price by doing a member or distributor registration.

She opted for retail pricing this time and said that once she was satisfied with the results she would do the registration. She was impressed with the fact that our company carried a one hundred percent money-back guarantee that was honored in the fifty plus countries where we carried on business.

Amazed to know that the company had been in business since 1950 and that I had been with them since March 1994; she added, "It must be an excellent company for you to have been with them so long." She then informed me that once she received benefits from the products she would be with us for life.

Hold On

"Great!" was my reply.

Having processed her order with the credit card information she provided we said our goodbyes and was of the phone. No sooner was the receiver returned to the cradle when "Rrrrring, rring, rring!"

With the receiver to my ear I answered with my usual, "Good day, Donna speaking, how may I help you?"

"How may I help you? How may I help you?" She repeated my question and asked, "Girl what happen to you? You know how long I have been holding on? You are something else with this crazy brain of yours; I said: 'I'm sure Donna forget I'm on the line'."

"Hahhhaaaa," laughingly I asked, "Why didn't you just hang up?"

"I kept thinking that you would be right back."

This became a ritual. If I put anyone on hold you might just as well forget about it because the moment I did was the very moment that I surely forgot t I was engaged in a conversation prior to the beep.

You know for sure not to ever hire me as a switchboard operator.

However, my dear friend never gave up on me. By no means was it deliberate. It took a while before I eventually realized that I could not multitask.

Be assured of this one fact: when we are on the line you have my undivided attention...guaranteed.

FYI: With a lot of nutrition support and getting to bed a bit earlier I am so much better now. I do return to the previous caller in very short order. This does not mean that I'm one hundred percent but then neither are you....hmmm.........but, in the future, we can have that privilege.

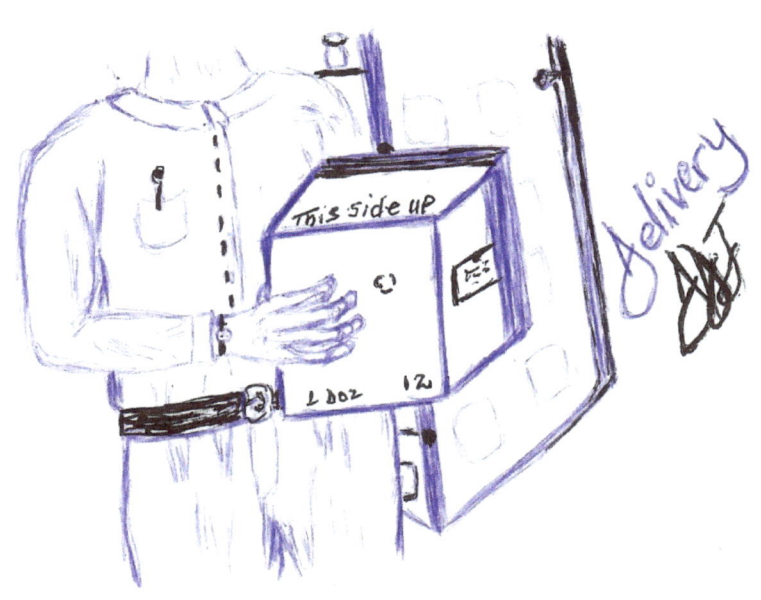

Chapter Twelve

Adrenalin rushed through my body as I pelted around the city from one appointment to the next. Having sold more products than anticipated inventory was running low. I needed to go to the office to replenish.

Within half an hour I was there, pulled up at the parking lot at the back. Once out the car, I hustled to the front of the quaint house that was the office; outside walls painted with a hint of green and a mild peach colored trim. I went up the four, brown, front stairs and headed inside. It was abuzz with distributors placing or collecting orders or just hanging around.

After a few salutations I headed to the restroom and surprisingly, was in and out in a blink. At the customer service counter I waited my turn to process my order; it was a large one.

Are you parked at the back? Sean asked.

"Yes."

"Ok, if you pull up to the back door, I'll put them in your trunk."

"Thanks, Sean. Really appreciate it." Although he was the only staff member in the office that day he was still very accommodating.

"Have a good day all." With those words I left the office, walked to the parking lot at the back, jumped in my car, got the engine tumbling, put her in gear, reversed a few feet, put her in drive, turned the steering to the left, drove out the parking lot and headed to my 1.30 pm appointment.

The traffic was not too bad at that time. I was a bit early but I preferred to get there and wait until time for the appointment rather than be late. I certainly did not want to ruffle any feathers with this customer after my dealings with him yesterday.

He had called and a rather unusual conversation ensued.

"Someone referred me to you. Are you Donna Dedier James?"

"Yes, I am. How may I help you?"

"Do you have a sister by the name of Jasmine?"

"Yes"

With that his tone changed. He sounded emotionally charged as he told me, "Well, I know Jasmine and she is a very nice person."

"For sure, she is a very nice person, and I'm happy you feel that way about my sister." I replied with a little bubble in my voice hoping to bring back calm to the caller.

"I'm sure you are not as nice your sister," he curtly responded.

Quite taken aback and before I could say another word he continued, "I don't want to do business with you. I want to do business with Jasmine. I would rather buy supplements from her than from you. I am sure you are not as pretty as she is either."

"Well sir, you may be right. Maybe I'm not as nice as she is or as pretty," I promptly replied. "It would then be so much better for you if you could get the supplements

Delivery

from her. The only problem with that is, she does not sell them, I do. That's why you were referred to me, and not to her. Now, seeing that you called me, it means you have a need that you feel I may be able to address and I would surely do my best to assist you, if, you are willing to let me know what issues you are facing. The person who referred you must have thought a lot about you and must also appreciate my ability to assist. Please thank them for me. I appreciate their confidence in me and their support and I certainly appreciate yours too." With that said, I waited.

Without another grouse over the fact that I was not Jasmine he quite meekly, as if a totally different person and maybe he was, went on to relate his situation. Recommendations were made, he placed the order and delivery was set for the following day.

Apart from the fact that I needed to be early for all my appointments, which habit I was working really hard to develop, it was for that particular reason that I was even more determined to be on time.

Turning of a secondary road and left onto Chacon street, traffic snarled for a little bit. It was good that the drop of location was only about a five minutes drive up the block.

A glance at the clock on the car stereo showed I had twenty minutes to play with before the appointment when, at that very moment, like a ton of bricks, it hit me: "You did not pick up the products. What is wrong with you?" Oh, my, goodness! So I was not early at all; I had no products to deliver.

In a mad dash I headed back to the office. I pulled up out front, flew out of the car, ran up the short flight of stairs, and dashed into the office like a mad woman calling out to Sean for the products.

Sean tilted his head, looked at me and said, "Donna, I went to the back and opened the door and waited for you to reverse and open your trunk so I could put the products in. I stood there with the boxes in my hand when you reversed, then you turned and drove off. I thought maybe you were going to angle the car differently or something, only to realize that you had gone out the driveway and up the street. I said: 'Donna crazy yes.' I waited for a few minutes because I thought you might realize and come back but you didn't. Oh, well, they are in front here. Where's your car?"

"It's out front. Would you bring them out for me please?"

"Sure."

With the products in tow I now raced out with not a single minute to spare and made it just in time.

Right at the front of the building stood the customer with his sunglasses and the sky blue, pin stripped shirt he said he would have been wearing. We exchanged greetings. I collected my $975.00 and he took his products. I thanked him for his business, got back into my vehicle and headed back to the office where they had a few more laughs at me for driving off without the products.

But the day was not finished. With the kids picked up from school and settled at home, I headed back into the city for a 6.00pm presentation. That went on for one hour. After which we packed our things and headed out the door. The manager and her husband did all the locks and together we all headed for the parking lot.

Trouble seemed to be looming, for now, in my car, I could not get it started. Several tries and nothing happened.

It was an automatic so we could not put it in drive, yet, we had to get it out onto the street because the gates had to be locked. I did not want to leave it there. With it on the street I would have been able to get either a mechanic or a tow truck that very night.

The manager's husband offered to help push the car outside. He was the only male on hand so he took the majority of the strain. What a job that was for the poor man, but no sooner had the car tires hit the street, when the lights went on in my brain. The reason the car would not start was because I had engaged the kill switch and had not disengaged it.

Boy oh boy! I felt badly, but they all had a good laugh in spite of the fact that I caused them to sweat bullets pushing the car outside.

Delivery

I am grateful they found it humorous and sadly I can't even remember the manager's husband's name; to him I say again, "Thanks a million."

Chapter Thirteen

It was about 10.30 in the morning when it occurred to me that I needed to get to the bank. I had loaned some money to a friend. The money just returned, later than expected, needed to be deposited into our bank account. It had just gone into the negative incurring a thirty five dollar non sufficient funds fee. Institutional thievery if you ask me.

Nonetheless, a call to the branch explaining the reason for the situation got the manager's approval for a reversal of the charge which would go into effect once the account was brought current. I wanted to be sure that that happened that very day.

With that in mind I had ample time to make that run and be back home by 2.30 in the afternoon. Nonetheless, rushing around the house at turtle speed it was already a little after 12 noon when I left the house.

It was a Wednesday; our meeting, our spiritual banquet, was held every Wednesday; so this was not the day when I should have been heading out of Brooklyn into Manhattan at such a late hour, but that was the case.

My branch was located on Lexington Avenue in New York City. I prayed that I would be out of the city before rush hour and with sufficient time to prepare dinner before Neil got in from work.

The B38 bus was not moving as fast as I would have liked, on its way into downtown Brooklyn. What did I expect? It was now close to 1 p.m. I had really left home way too late; but also too late now for regrets.

Downstairs in the subway, the number four uptown train pulled into the station just as my feet landed on the platform, and before I knew it, I had connected to the number six train and was at my stop in New York City.

Oblivious of the constant beat of the 'greatest city' in the world, I all but ran across the street past FedEx Kinko's and into the bank. The atmosphere was always relaxed at that branch, a line almost nonexistent and the staff always warm; more accommodating in my eyes than the branch closer to me on Fulton Street, downtown Brooklyn.....tell me why? Huuhhmm!!!!

Business was quickly cared for by the manager and, in two twos, was on my way. Passed two buildings, crossed one street and down into the subway; my metro card swiped and speedily I headed for the number six downtown train. The wait was not too long, so together with some after work commuters, I entered the train. A few stops later we connected to the downtown number four train.

We had gone only a little ways with the train about to pull off from the third stop when I heard over the train's intercom: "Stand clear of the closing doors!" Quickly I glanced across the platform and spotted a number six train. Immediately, something clicked in my brain: my feet sprang into action and, with an upward sprint I was off my seat and dashed out of the number four train and into the number six.

Stand Clear

Letting out a sigh of relief for having made it before either of the trains doors had closed, I sat down. Huh? At that moment I realized my dilemma. Looking around the train car it became obvious to me that I was its only occupant.

Looking ahead and behind at the other cars, with growing dismay I realized not only was the car that I occupied was empty, rather, the entire train was empty save the driver, of course. But before I could collect my thoughts the train had pulled out of the station.

What in the world was I doing on this train? Why did I get off the number four train in the first place? Somehow, when the voice on that other train said: "Stand clear of the closing doors!" it sent a signal, wrong as it was, to my brain to get off and hop onto the train across the platform.

Now this number six train was going to 'I don't know where.' The headline of the following day's newspaper flashed across my brain: "Woman found dead on train." In my mind's eye the drama unfolded: there I sat scrunched on a seat in the dark, hot train parked somewhere underground, the driver long gone off the train, now at home with his family, oblivious of the fact that a lone, female passenger was left there overnight to die.

Worse yet I saw myself fighting of some lunatic who eventually, well, I stopped there in my imagination but I still ended up on the front of the newspaper as a woman who was killed on the downtown number four train.

I prayed to Jehovah for help. I needed to get to my meeting. I had prepared well and was looking forward to the spiritual banquet he had prepared, and for the fellowship with my loving brothers and sisters. My husband and family would be worried. No one knew where I was.

As I supplicated Jehovah to help me maintain my composure I began to think about what was needed to be done in order to alert the driver that someone besides himself was on board. I looked at the sliding doors at either end of the car I was in. "Maybe I could walk through from car to car until I got to him at the front of the train," I thought. However, being directionally challenged

I was hard pressed to figure out which end that was.

Notwithstanding, the very thought scared the daylights out of me. I had seen it done in real life and on television and every time my heart made an unsuccessful somersault imagining me doing same thing; "Not I said the fly, surely won't happen." In any event that was now illegal after the many fatalities of young and not so young alike.

I took some slow deep breaths and thought about what a friend had told me years ago. I looked for the emergency brakes that she said she had pulled when she had got on the train but her husband had not because the doors had closed so fast. Ok, I found the brakes but debated: "Pull it or pull it not? Pull it? Pull it not?"

"Pull it," I thought; but what would happen I did not know.

Would the driver hear a siren or something? Would he stop and come to check or would he say something over the intercom? I prayed again, then reached up and pulled on the brakes. "Duh!" It just occurred to me that brakes equal slow down or stop. Suddenly the train began to slow down in the tunnel. My heart raced as I sat to await whatever the result would be. But after what seemed like an eternity the train started moving again.

Claustrophobia seemed determined to set in but I would not allow it; so I earnestly prayed to my heavenly father for his holy spirit to strengthen me. With that I got up and pulled on the brakes again. Shortly thereafter the trained proceeded to slow down a second time. I am not sure if it did come to a full stop but even if it did where was I going to get off? We were still in the darkened tunnel but just like earlier it pulled off again.

"Okay, now I'm really finished," I thought to myself, convinced that no one was coming to look for me. Praying to Jehovah again I became determined not to die like this without a fight and so began to think positively about what I needed do to get out when, "Wow!" out of the darkened tunnel shone a glimmer of light. Brighter and brighter the light became as gradually we emerged from the darkened hollow and before I knew it the train had pulled into a station, and voila, the doors opened onto a well lit

Stand Clear

platform.

Without a second thought I got up and fled out of the train, then went about my business of getting back onto the right train and headed home.

Back in Brooklyn my appreciation heightened for the inestimable privilege bestowed upon me. Yes, I was totally elated to be in the land of the living and be able to get to my meeting and praise my God.

Why my brain responded the way it did to that announcement I have no idea but I do try to stop and think before I step into or out of a train.

As for you my dear reader, train, bus, car or other be sure you do the same.

The Plane Plane....

Tickets

Chapter Fourteen

It was another busy day, trying to tie up all loose ends before flying out the next day from Port of Spain, Trinidad & Tobago to San Francisco, USA.

My bonus check had just come in so I needed to deposit that at the bank. We also wanted a few travelers' checks to use, for safety, instead of cash. If they got lost or stolen they would be replaced.

With that cared for, and all scheduled deliveries completed, we wrapped up the day with a presentation. When that was over we packed up the display, put all my paraphernalia in my trunk and for a change headed home well before sunset.

Constant laughter could have been heard throughout our journey as I dropped off one after another of the four distributors, who rode with me, at their respective residences. Finally, around 5.30 pm I pulled into my driveway breathing a sigh of relief.

Home at last to get packed and sort things out for the kids for the week. Jackie was there and a great help. By the time I was ready to take her home she had the kids showered and dressed, Akeyla had all homework done, and lunches were prepared and packed in the refrigerator for them for school the following day.

We were all in for an early start that day. Neil had sat down with us and outlined how things were to be handled that morning we were traveling, and how things were to be cared for with the kids and Jackie for the week.

Jackie was to spend the week with the kids. My brother in law, Carlos, would have my car for the week. He agreed to get the kids every morning and take them to school and pick them up after school and bring them home. All was set.

After dropping Jackie at her home that night, I returned to get myself together. With travel clothes and other essentials all set I headed for a shower, shampoo and a quick conditioner to my hair; then a roller set. No sooner was this done when the phone rang.

Glancing at the clock it was 11.45 pm. Leah was on the other end. "You all set she asked?"

"Just about," I replied. "I'm hoping to get a few hours sleep but I have to blow dry my hair and I need a cup of tea before I retire."

"Ok, let me ask you, did you miss anything this evening?"

"Not really, like what?"

Very calmly she asked, "Like your bag, do you have it?"

"What bag?" I asked all confused as to where she was going with this.

"Your work bag? Do you have it?"

"Yes, I think I have it?"

"Ok, why don't you go and check and see."

I surely checked.

"Oh boy, I could not find it anywhere, and our tickets are in that bag."

"You forgot it at the office," she said. "It's a good thing I noticed it when we were leaving and they were about to

Tickets

lock up. I said, 'that looks like Donna's bag'."

"You are good; I don't know how you could tell with so many others like it. Wow! Wow! Wow! My goodness, I hate to think what the situation would have been like in the morning had you not noticed it. Hummm! That was Jehovah, Bless the God of Abraham, Isaac and Jacob from time indefinite even forever! Thank you, Jehovah. Thank you too, Leah. It's a good thing you went to the office after me. I'll get it from you early in the morning on my way up to Arima, a little after 6.00am, after I pick up Jackie. Thanks a lot."

On that note we said our goodnights. The kids and Neil were fast asleep, and I needed to head there too, but not before I blow dried my hair and had my cup of tea.

It was five o'clock in the morning when Neil roused me from slumber. By 5.30 he was showered and dressed and headed out the door but not before reminding me, "Please leave at six to get Carlos so we could be on time for the flight."

He had picked up Jackie and brought her over and immediately headed to Arima. The plan was that he would take his car up to my mom's home and park it in her garage. Then I would leave home at six o'clock drive up to my brother in law in Mausica, a little suburban area on the outskirts of the borough of Arima, pick him up, then drive up to my mom's and get Neil. Carlos would then drive my car to take us to the airport.

Simple enough plan, but unknown to Neil, before heading to Carlos, I had to go over to Leah in Trincity to get my bag that contained our airline tickets.

It was ten minutes after six when I headed out the door with Akeyla in tow, taking her for the ride, so she could make the run with us to the airport. With the pedal to the metal I gunned up the road onto the highway towards Leah.

A left turn took me into the Trincity housing development area where all roads looked alike and so did the majority of the houses. The street all had flowery names like Carnation etcetera. For the life of me I could not remember the name of the street Leah lived on, although I had been there a 'million' times, so finding it should have been no big deal.

Quite contrary to my thought, I found myself on a street where I thought she lived but her house was not there. Okay, it must be the next street, so out one street and into the next, but her house was not there either.

Hmmm, nerves felt closed to getting jangled; where was her house located? This was no new place to me; had been there at least once a week. I asked Akeyla to pray to Jehovah to help me find the right street while I prayed to stay calm.

Out of that second street and into another, panic was really beginning to set in. Those were not the days where everyone and his brother had a cell phone. What a blessing, as I drove onto that third Street, there was a lady outside in her front yard talking on her cordless landline.

I pulled up at her gate and anxiously waited for her to finish her conversation, and almost incoherently attempted to explain to her my predicament.

"Miss good morning, sorry to bother you, I have a flight to catch at 8.45 this morning and my tickets are in my bag that I have to collect at my friend and I am so confused I can't find her house although I know where she lives and have been at her so often can I please use your phone to call her to get directions how to get to her please, please or else I'll miss the flight and I have to pick up my husband in Arima to go on that flight too."

I am not sure if she had time to respond but I all but snatched the phone from her hand, called Leah and asked her to speak to the woman and give her the directions so she could physically point to where I had to go to get to her. With that I hastily put the phone to the woman's ear so she could get the directions for me. I thanked her and left.

Two minutes was all it took to get to Leah. She was outside with the bag which I grabbed and headed back onto the highway up to Jasmine's house to pick up her husband. Another left turn off the highway onto Mausica Road feeling that all was going well with tickets in hand.

No one had told Akeyla that she was in for a ride of a

Tickets

lifetime and certainly no one told me that the drama had only just begun. Halfway into the ride up Mausica Road it occurred to me that I was once again on a wrong road or was I?

Completely turned around I could not for the life of me figure out where Jasmine lived. They all seemed to live on the left so another left turn into what I felt might have been her street and, nope, it was not. Now I was really beginning to panic; absolutely clueless about which way to go.

The best thing, I thought, was to go back to the highway and get my bearing. I ignored that thought went to the main road and turned left and went onto another secondary road running parallel to Mausica Road. A few minutes into the drive I realized that made no sense, it was a wild goose chase, so I got back out onto the main road.

There I got a grip on my senses and pulled to the side. I told Akeyla we were going to say a prayer to Jehovah to help me to think straight and for wisdom to know what would be the best course of action. No sooner had we finished the prayer when it came to me to go over to Paula's* home on the other side of the Eastern Main Road, not far from where we were parked. She would know where Jasmine lived.

We drove and turned to get on the other side of the street. This time it was a right turn, and then another right turn, and right on track we were at Paula's where she shared a missionary home with Jeanie.*

"Wheeeww!" Paula was home but, to my dismay, she did not know exactly where Jasmine lived. However, before my chin could drop to the floor she said, "Jeanie knows, she studies with Jasmine. She's inside, so let me get her."

What a welcomed sight as out came Jeanie in her night gown. "Yes," she said in her very gentle voice "I could take you there, the only thing I would have to change out of my night gown."

"Oh, no, we won't have time for that. We are trying to catch the 8.45 flight. I'll take you in the car and bring you right back, please, if you don't mind." She lovingly complied.

With that we sped off to Jasmine. From this direction we turned right into her street, and lo and behold, pulled up in front of her door thanks to Jeanie's expert direction. Carlos had just stepped out the front door about to head out his gate.

"I was just about to leave," he said. "I thought you had changed your plans."

"Are you kidding me? Get in Carlos, let's go. Thank Jehovah for Jeanie, I could not find the house."

Now, with a u turn we were set to get Neil and to the airport but what time was it? It was now 7.55 am. Jeanie had to be dropped off but she was back on the other side of the Eastern Main Road about five minutes away which now seemed so very far.

"Jeanie, I know I promised to take you back home but if I do we would never get there in time for the flight. The main problem is that if we miss this flight we will also miss the connecting flight from Miami to San Francisco. If I drop you at your corner on the main road would you mind, please, walking home from there? It's not very far in, would you mind? I hate to do this to you. You were so kind to come with me but we still have to go to Arima and pick up my husband, which will take us at least twenty minutes, then to get to the airport."

By this time I was at her corner and still apologizing to her. She looked down at her night gown and said, "Well, I have never walked the street in my nightie before, and I don't want you to miss your flight, so I guess this will be a first," and with that she, laughingly, obliged and got out the car.

Naturally, we all laughed, but in hind sight that was a very, very, very selfish act on my part. I was late, not her. Certainly, I remembered to write her a thank you card on my return. But for now the saga continued.

Exactly 8.10 am we pulled up in front my mother's home. Neil was out front waiting patiently. He offered to drive.

"We have a little over half an hour before the flight leaves and you won't get us there in time. Please let me

Tickets

drive; I'll get us there quickly and safely so, please, don't panic. I know I drive fast but I'm also very cautious, so please let me do this." He agreed and with that we took off.

8.25 am, we pulled up at the drop of point at the airport, kissed and hugged our baby girl, handed the keys to Carlos, Neil had already given him money for gas etc., grabbed our luggage and headed to the ticketing counter.

Just in the nick of time, we got there with only eighteen minutes left before takeoff. That part was a breeze as the counter was empty. Now, with boarding passes in hand, we were about to go through to the security area when the announcement: "flight number so and so, due for departure at 8.45 am to Miami, Florida, is delayed."

I could not believe my ears. "Are you serious? All this and it's delayed? Well, at least we made it on time."

"I am hungry. I am going to go to the food barn next to the airport and get my favorite chicken sandwich. Do you want one?" Neil asked.

"No thanks honey. Do you think it's wise to do that? It's a good five minutes' walk away, and they always have a line."

"Don't worry; I'll be back in time." With that Neil went his way, which left me a bit nervous. The thought of him getting stuck in a long line over there and us missing the flight was troublesome. I had had enough drama for one morning.

All this time I had forgotten about Leah and Dennis; they were also booked on that same 8.45 flight. I had not caught a glimpse of them and just when I was trying to figure out where they could be a gentleman approached.

"Are you Donna Dedier James?"

"Yes."

"Okay, come with me; we have to get you on another flight right away so you won't miss your connecting flight. I understand that you have to be in San Francisco for a specific time for an event."

Just as I feared; it was too good to be true. We thought we were late, and then we were early, now, with Neil gone for a sandwich, it appeared that we would be late once again. "Oh dear, my husband is here too, he went to the food barn."

"Don't worry, I'll find him."

"Do you know what he looks like? He's wearing a beige long sleeve shirt..." before I could finish the sentence he assured me that he'll find him.

"Go quickly," he said you have barely enough time to board. Go to gate number so and so...your husband will meet you there."

On my way to the gate I met Leah and Dennis. They were the ones who had taken care of that, otherwise we would all have missed the connecting flight and would not have arrived in San Francisco until the following evening. We, now, headed through security to go to the gate.

I was concerned about Neil, how would the man find him? He did not know my husband. How did he know what I looked like so that he came straight up to me?

Just then Neil appeared, huffing and puffing that he was looking for me where he left me but couldn't find me. The man found him and gave him the same information.

"I couldn't wait for you. I was told to go straight to the gate or we would not get on the flight. Let's be grateful the guy found you. Let's board, we're the last to get on."

So, presto, before we knew it, we had boarded the plane and were in the air on our way to our destination. What a morning!

I never remembered to ask how the man at the airport knew what we looked like. And it only just occurred to me that I could have collected my bag from Leah at the airport. Why did not one of us think about that and saved ourselves all that drama, and more so I would have spared Jeanie the walk down her street in her night gown. That was really thoughtless of me. Jeanie I am sorry.

*Names have been changed.

Bridge over very cold waters.

Chapter Fifteen

Having read thus far, this comedic drama in particular is a project for you to figure out what's wrong with my brain; so here goes....

Being relatively new in New York it was my first time travelling on the J train without husband, child, children or friend. The car was fairly full of people heading into the 'city that never sleeps.' Crossing the Williamsburg Bridge was part of the normal route for that train from Brooklyn to Manhattan and vise versa. On that crisp November day I boarded the train at the Kosciusko station in Bedford Stuyvesant in Brooklyn.

Having pulled up at the following five stations we then came onto the bridge. Keeping totally alert and focused was the only way for me to be certain not to go past my stop. The train, now about mid way on the bridge, suddenly began to slow down. In a moment of mental

Bridge Over

confusion I wondered: why?

It then appeared to me that the driver was trying to put me out right there on the bridge. Why was he trying to put me out? This was not my stop so why would he want to do that? I felt that at any moment the train would come to a halt and I would be expected to get off.

I looked around at the other passengers. Everyone seemed quite nonchalant. No one else appeared to be preparing to exit the train; not one. It seemed I was the only one the driver wanted to put out here, in the middle of nowhere.

Looking through the windows to the outside of the train onto the bridge, I tried to locate an area where I would safely be able to stand when he put me off the train. Any fall of the bridge would be a long deathly drop into the very cold waters of the river way, way below.

There were cars going by on the right side of the suspended railing that made a separation between the road they were on and the train tracks. How safe would I be out there? This looked rightly like a 'bridge over very cold, troubled waters.'

My destination, Essex Street/Delancey Street, was the first stop on the other side of this bridge. How would I get to my destination from there? Would I be able to walk on the bridge? From my vantage point it appeared to have no foot traffic at all nor was there a path that I could see which would have allowed same. Panic was beginning to slowly set in so I prayed to Jehovah for help. Suddenly the train picked up speed. "Oh wow!" I sighed to relieve myself.

Just when I thought I was out of danger the train began to slow down again. Why did the driver feel this desperate need to get me of the train? This was the question racking my mind. I never rang a bell and indeed there was no bell to ring. I hadn't asked him to put me out here and indeed I did not even know what the driver looked like. In fact had not seen the individual nor spoken with the individual so why make me his target?

Before my thoughts could take me any further down this dead end road, a gush of relief coursed through my veins as the train picked up speed again. And in a moment's breath we pulled into the Essex street station. To be certain no one had to ask me to leave. Like flood waters after torrential showers I speedily followed the rush of folks out the opened train doors onto the platform.

Through the turnstile, as I headed up those seemingly never ending flight of subway stairs, my legs didn't seemed to burn as they usually would. My face, raised to the drink in the bright sunlight, eagerly welcomed, and gladly took a deep breath of the overly polluted, lower east side air. I'll take that for now, thank you! Paradise is on its way.

Your verdict please....

Chapter Sixteen

The winter was proving to be an extremely snowy one. It was January and the snow storms were coming fast and furious. Already there had been five for the season dumping almost a foot of snow each time.

Out came the sunshine but did little to melt away what was left of the mounds of snow piled up from the last storm. Interestingly in spite of the golden rays the temperature outside was extremely frigid, unusual for the lower New York area.

Inside was altogether a different story feeling nice and toasty with the thermostat set at seventy two degrees Fahrenheit. But this was Monday, my stay at home day and I always enjoyed that.

The ideal would have been to get an early start so as to

Break In

derive the greatest benefit possible from the day; but having slept way too late the outlook for much productivity was very, very grim. Nonetheless, my mood was not affected; this would be my do-me day.

A spinach omelet with crushed red pepper, parsley, a little cilantro, sea salt, purple onion and a little bit of diced green pepper cooked in coconut oil was just the breakfast the doctor ordered. That would do for me today instead of my usual protein shake.

Nothing would have been better with that than my own home made, gourmet, whole grain bread of which I had none. If you hadn't baked in a while how you would have your own homemade bread? Figure that out if you can.

Well, with no bread I settled for six, crispy, bran and oats crackers. Having added a hot cup of peppermint tea, with a little unsweetened organic, vanilla flavor, soy milk to the mix, that went down just right, and I was as happy as pappy.

Enthralled by simple pleasures this seemed to be set to be somewhat of my one day kind of holiday. Yup, it doesn't take much to make me happy. No need for Puerto Vallarta or Montpellier. Home alone with some hot of the stove, highly seasoned, homemade fried chicken breast on a plate, on my lap, with a knife and fork, and my feet plumped up on an ottoman and you would have made a happy camper out of me...easy.

Now showered and dressed I felt ready to take on the rest of the day. It would be best to run to the bank before sitting down at the computer to work on this book. My little burnt orange colored table at the top of the stairs was home to mother and daughter and father and son family photos and the shiny black outside, white inside, six inch tall hexagon shaped vase that housed winter gloves and sunglasses. Underneath sat two shelves for shoes and boots. From there I grabbed my inexpensive supposed shearling lined, supposed to keep my feet warm, short winter boots.

Just then the storm door opened. What sounded like Neil's key being inserted into the lock drifted upstairs. In short order you would hear the thump of his shoes coming up the stairs. They must have had an early day today. It was just about 12.30 pm so that would have been extra early for him.

With one side boot on and the other in hand I waited but a moment for his appearance. Instead, there was silence. Suddenly, what sounded like a shoulder thump against the door jolted me. Did he unlock the door but could not get it opened? Was the door stuck? That could happen....some swelling of the door due to the cold weather etcetera.

Looking over the railing I saw that the door chain was off so there was no obvious physical reason why it would not open. Without hesitation I called Neil on his cell phone to find out if he was having trouble opening the door. To my surprise he was at work. Who then was at the door? I explained to him what had just transpired and he encouraged me to hang up and call the police. He was not working from the shop today so he was quite some distance away.

Someone had attempted to break in. I headed to the window next to my little table. From there I would be able to see the outside stairs and the door. Moving the long green window box with my rosemary, Italian parsley and basil plants I pushed the widow up, pushed up the screen and looked out. There was no one there. Looking out into the street there was not even a delivery truck like Federal Express or United Parcel Service or United States Postal Service. Yet the sounds heard had been absolutely distinct. That was not my imagination.

Hesitatingly I called 911 as Neil had instructed.

"What's the problem?" They asked.

I explained the situation: "I think someone might have been trying to break in." They took all the necessary information and gave assurance that the police would be there shortly.

Could it be that my neighbor and friend LaChaughn had been at my door dropping of mail? One phone call to her answered that question. Absolutely not as she, like Neil, was at work.

She was very concerned. She too suggested calling the

Break In

police but that had already been done.

"Are you scared?" she asked. "Do you want me to come over?" she was ready to spring into action.

She worked close by but I didn't want her to have to leave work or to put her in any danger but she was not afraid. Feeling a little unnerved maybe it was best to accept her support so I said, "Ok, if it's not too much trouble you can come; I would appreciate that."

Life can be unpredictable. Reflecting at that moment of how easy things can go awry when my phone rang; it was LaChaughn letting me know she was at my door. Hurriedly I went down stairs, looked through the peep hole to confirm that it was indeed her. Excitedly I pulled the door opened; to my great surprise, sitting between the inner door and the storm door was a small package.

"What in the world is this?" I asked astonishingly, picking up the itsy bitsy box. LaChaughn laughed as I held up the package.

"How crazy is this? I had completely forgotten that I had been expecting a UPS delivery," I remarked.

She asked: "You didn't come down and looked though the peep hole when you heard the noise earlier?"

"I was afraid," I answered, "in case the assailant had a gun and heard me inside the door and riddled me with bullets. People crazy now, you know. Girl, I figured on playing it safe by just looking out the window from upstairs,"

"Oh boy, how our brains go to work....oh well, you are safe so that's good," she said.

We both laughed and she headed back to work.

Yes, UPS had fulfilled their end: they delivered. There was no bell rung, not once, not twice so how would I have known that they were at the door? Not to mention either how quickly they must have driven off or how slowly I moved before looking through the window. Remember, I looked out and saw nothing. As a matter of fact I had also looked out the front window and the window at the other side of the living room too.

Oh well, all is well that ends well and so I thought when suddenly, "ding dong, ding dong" went the sound of the door bell. Without hesitation, I opened the window and stuck my head through only to see two men in blue. Oh oh! Immediately I began apologizing. They asked me to come downstairs. This I did.

"I am so sorry," I said explaining to them what had happened.

"That's fine!" one of them responded. "We are happy for these kinds of calls. We are glad that you are ok."

The other one continued, "It is better that you call us if you suspect something and it turns out to be nothing than you don't call us and the end is tragic."

He added, "Don't apologize! We are just happy you are safe. Have yourself a good day."

Merrily, I replied, "And a very good day to you guys too and be safe." On that note I went inside finished getting dressed and went my cherry way to do a 'teenie weenie' bit of banking. So it was no 'break in'....but whenever your days are too busy just be sure to take a break out...I mean.....get some fresh air.....

Break In

If you haven't had a chance to look up today here's an awesome view.

Winter Sky 2014
Donna Dedier James

Come Out With Your Hands Up!

Chapter Seventeen

The driveway was a bit narrow, but once you got through our gate you were greeted with a huge, concrete paved yard at the front and side of the new two story four apartment house. The two upstairs apartments were not completed. We occupied downstairs left and a few month later an older couple took up residence to the right.

We could park much where ever we pleased, however, when we were in for the night we parked the car at the extreme, front corner of the yard. The car would be put to sit tight to the wall in front of us and tight to the wall at our right. Car theft was very common in Trinidad at that time; so you made it not an easy task for anyone attempting to illegally remove your car from your premises.

It was for that reason, that on entering the gate, I

turned the car towards the right and drove all the way up to the wall that separated our property from our next door neighbor. In doing so I also pulled in close to the wall on my right. This left just enough room to exit the car but one had to be careful in opening the door not to smash it against the wall.

The children had thoroughly enjoyed their jaunts for the day and so it was a thrill to see, very rarely at that, Yohance get out of the car without coercion. My twenty year old, 'baby' sister Arlene was a favorite of both Yohance and Akeyla. Together we had 'funned' him to exhaustion so he hustled his way out the car and shuffled in a hurry towards the apartment door. Akeyla and Arlene trailed behind him.

Earlier that day the drive down to Chaguaramas was exhilarating. No sea bathing that time just taking in the scenery, enjoying, the smell of sea water, the intermittent sound of waves crashing ashore, and stopping to visit family in the area. Over at Auntie Jenny's, my older sister, we had a bathroom break and took time to laugh a bit.

We always had something to laugh about which more often than not included ourselves. We were indeed a funny bunch; we were forever laughing at each other. Kelly Ann, Curvin or Keston may have been doing the "Hance" (this was Yohance's permanent dance....popular with us - don't know why it never made it to the big screen) which got everyone laughing including Yohance himself.

Arlene had fun names for all of us based on our personality, manner of speaking or other nuances. No wonder Akeyla started writing about us at age six or seven. She figured that there had to be a book about this crazy family, and so, she astutely gave it the title "Meet the Dediers." I don't think she got very far with it but no doubt if completed would be a bestseller. Do the book Akeyla, do the book!

Louise our mother had been the chief comedienne. She had the knack for having you cracking up so it must have been for sure that we were her progeny. Laughter was embedded in our DNA.

Well, it wasn't funny that Yohance deliberately

Come Out

knocked over Tom's bowl of shelled pigeon peas but most of them were laughing anyway. Yohance was not thrilled since he had to help pick up much of all those little pea grains. With that cared for we headed home.

As the earth travelled on its daily journey around the sun it graciously left the last of sunlight behind. Twilight was now replaced by the light of the other beauty, the moon, "the faithful witness" in the night sky. Though not a full moon, it still gave a bit of light as they headed to the door. There Yohance and Akeyla waited for Arlene to unlock it.

Still in the car I turned the ignition key shutting off the engine. Just then my cell phone rang and I took the call before putting on the 'kill switch' and the steering wheel lock.

Leah was on the other end but before she could finish her sentence I turned my head towards the apartment door in response to Arlene's urgent call. Yohance and Akeyla were walking through the door into the apartment whilst Arlene with body turned towards the car was calling out to me in a whispering shout: "Donna, there's a man walking up the driveway with a gun." She sounded terrified.

I motioned her to go inside and lock the door. At the same time I sent my window glass all the way up. With Leah on the other end of the phone I told her what Arlene had just said as I crouched down in the car. She told me to stay on the phone while she called the police."

I heard her as she spoke with them on her land line. She came back to me to get information, address etcetera, to give to the police. Finally she told me:

"They are on their way so I'll stay on the phone with you until they get there." Then she suggested that she had better call Arlene to let her know that she was on the phone with me and that she had called the police. Arlene told her the man had gone next door so she relayed that information to me.

After what seemed like forever there was a beep on my phone from an incoming call. Placing Leah on hold I took the call; a sigh of relief, it was the police. They had pulled up out front and wanted me to come out.

Are they crazy? I told them, "I can't come out. I'm in the car. The man went to the unfinished house next door, he has a gun. Do you want me to get shot?"

The officer then told me to drive my car towards the gate, but I refused for fear the perpetrator would shoot me. After going back and forth with them they suggested I put on my car lights. I then reversed it a little bit whilst trying to keep my head down in case a bullet was fired. Arlene had also put on the outside light for the apartment.

The cops were more scared than we were; what a thing! Finally, with my car lights on, two cops walked up the driveway, one with a loudspeaker shouting: "Come out with your hands up! You there in the unfinished house come out with your hands up!"

By this time another officer drove the police vehicle partially up the driveway with the lights on full blast. The two officers came closer to the unfinished house next door whilst the one with the loudspeaker spoke again: "You there inside this unfinished house, this is the police. We know you are in there; come out with your hands up!"

"Don't let us have to bring the troops in there for you or it could get ugly; come out with your hands up!"

By this time I was stooped on the back seat of the car, peering over the seat at the goings on with the police. I had rolled the window down a tad for air, and to be able to hear what was being said.

Just then, a tall figure emerged out of the darkness of the unfinished house next door. Gradually he came into the light; the apparent predator, bare backed with his hands up in the air, face bewildered.

The police asked him, "What were you doing in there and where is the gun?

He grimaced, obviously confused as to the goings on. "I am the watchman for this building, I have no gun. Ask these people, they know me; they see me here every day. Where's the lady who drives this car? They all know me. What is all this about?"

The police called out on the loudspeaker: "Ma'am please come out and see if you can identify this man?"

With that I got out of the car and slowly walked over to

Come Out

the police. I wanted to laugh.

"Of course I know him, he's from next door. My sister called out that she saw a man coming up the driveway with a gun. She did not know it was you in the dark; she did not make you out. I'm soooo sorry."

The poor man squinted his eyes, looked at me in amazement and asked: "A gun? Lady I don't even own a gun. You know I'm the watchman here. I went to the shop (store) to buy a loaf of bread."

By this time Arlene was outside with us and we all apologized profusely. No hard feelings, the guy went back to his post and the police to their precinct.

We felt badly that we had put the man through such an ordeal; but to this day we can't stop laughing at that. And to think, people think it's my brain that has a problem; it's everybody's brain.

Arlene saw a loaf of bread and thought it was a gun. Now how do you slice that? Hold the butter please.

Until next time....don't forget, sit in your rocker and think up your stories and, maybe you can have us laughing as I hope we gave you enough things to "bust your belly" laughing about.

What you may not know

Ayodele.....Joy enters the house

Chinkee.....Trinidadian word means really small

Dial ..... A clock that is an historical landmark

Tamarind....An amazing, tropical fruit with a hard, brown, outer shell. The fruit can be sweet or sour in taste with a brown, hard, glossy seed. Try the sweet one first if you have never had it before.
The fruit can be used in a variety of ways: Mixed with sugar you can make tamarind balls....oh so good. Mixed with a little baking soda, a little salt, hot pepper(to taste), and some sugar and you get a delicious, tangy desert with a hint of fizz; almost like a carbonated, fun snack...I have no name for that....maybe someone else has a name for it but I don't; just love the thing. I just love it, sweet or sour.

Tamarind Balls.....
The fruit of the tamarind all 'mushed' together with salt, pepper, and lots of sugar into a gooey mixture. It is then separated into to smaller pieces that is then rolled into balls...uuhhmm, uuhhmm, uuhhmm,

Tantie ......Caribbean word for Auntie

Titivating....... Moving around doing nothing

Sugar Cake......A mixture of grated coconut, sugar and flavoring cooked on the stove then dropped by spoonful onto a sheet to cool then to be enjoyed. It could be soft or crunchy

Look out for my next book
"Toothbrushes on the ceiling"

Did you enjoy this book? Please recommend it to your friends; and like us on Facebook - leave a review if you can. Facebook page: Memoirs of a forgetful mind

To find out about bulk ordering
Go to our web site www.wilaf.com

About the author

Donna has a writing style that is totally her own and is extremely engaging. Her refusal to take herself too seriously is reflected in her writings. As a devoted wife, and mother of one boy and one girl, her family means the world to her. She loves people. More important to her than all else is her relationship with her God, Jehovah. She is keenly interested in creation and can always be seen taking photos of the sky and clouds, a flower, a neighbor's dog or cat, your feet, or even a piece of log. She sees beauty in almost everything. She laughs a lot and she keeps you laughing.

www.ingramcontent.com/pod-product-compliance
Lightning Source LLC
Chambersburg PA
CBHW042340150426
43196CB00001B/3